T0063251

No More Closed Doors

Christina T. Nance

authorHOUSE®

AuthorHouse™
1663 Liberty Drive
Bloomington, IN 47403
www.authorhouse.com
Phone: 1 (800) 839-8640

Published by AuthorHouse 09/11/2015

ISBN: 978-1-5049-3286-8 (sc)
ISBN: 978-1-5049-3287-5 (e)

Print information available on the last page.

This book is printed on acid-free paper.

First giving honor to God for saving me. Thank you for allowing me to see another day and allowing my voice to be heard.

I would like to give thanks to my mother Ronnett, my grandmother Betty and my great grandma Madea. Thanks for the conversations and encouraging words. Thanks for supporting me through every journey life has lead me. I love you all more than words can explain.

To my aunts, great aunts, uncles and relatives, thank you for being by side and helping me overcome the darkest chapter in my life.

To my siblings Sophia, Camellia, Loriel, Malisa, Anthony and Michael thank you all for loving me and being there for me. Through all our ups and downs, smiles and frowns, we still standing. I love you all unconditionally.

To my dear cousin Jasmine, you are more like a big sister than anything. Thank you for allowing me to sit on your couch and talk, thank you for listening and most of all, thank you for having faith in me and pushing me forward.

To Carole, thank you for the opportunity to speak with the commission and guiding me on the right path.

To my Pastor and First Lady Rollerson, thank you for being there for me and opening the church doors for my voice to be heard. I want to also give thanks to Mr. and Mrs. Mackey for being there for me. Thanks to a good friend of my mother, Tasha, for being there for me in her absences and to my good sister/friend Ashlynn, thank you for being there every step of the way.

I would like to thank my husband James for being by my side through my darkest days, hours, minutes and seconds. To my son Malik and daughter Jayla, thank you for showing me how to love someone other than myself. Love you both to the moon and back. My step children, I love you all like I gave birth to you.

This book is dedicated to anyone suffering with Mental Illness. God will stand with you through your darkest moment and HE will stand with you during your brightest moment. Keep the faith.

One love,

Christina

"I can do all things through Christ that strengthens ME!"

~Philippians 4:13~

I remind myself of this daily. It keeps me motivated outside of my kids. It reminds me that no matter what I am going through I can and will make it.

Every day is a constant struggle, but through the grace of God, I pull through. Many days I sit back and wonder why, why did God save me?

I constantly think about the would of's, could of's, should of's and what if's, but HE redirects my focus to concentrate on the I can's, I will's and I have's.

I have a wonderful support system and I will be forever grateful for that. Not many can say the same. My support consist of God, my husband, my kids, family and friends.

The little things I once took for granted, I now cherish. The hugs from my kids, their kisses, their "I love you mommy" every morning, the daily text messages asking if they could go somewhere even to the calls of wanting a ride somewhere. Simple things like that

Healing takes time and although there are still nights I have nightmares, I am finally at a point where I can sleep through the night without sleeping pills. I find myself question my own thoughts asking if anyone notice change, were we all blind to the signs or was I that good at covering up my cry for help?

My biggest fear is going down that dark hole again. I pray to God daily that he heals me properly, but I know the healing will be in his time and not mine. I know that he walk with me everyday and that I have a purpose in life.

I am sharing my testimony with you all to bring awareness of Mental Illness and Suicide Prevention. Many of us suffer from some form of Mental Illness, whether it be depression, bi-polar, anxiety disorders, mood disorders, schizophrenia/psychotic disorders, dementia disorders, eating disorders, drugs/street drugs, phobia, paranoia and the list goes on.

Bringing awareness to my community, the black community is so important to me. Many of us was raised hearing "what goes on in my house, stays in my house" or "child, ain't nothing wrong with you, go play" or "I'll call so and so and will have the church pray for you" or "don't be out there airing our dirty laundry."

It is time to stop hiding behind closed doors and start walking through and acknowledging the illness many of us suffer from.

Suicide

Definition:

- the action of killing oneself intentionally
- a person who does this
- a course of action that is disastrously damaging to oneself or one's own interest
- relating to or denoting a violent act or attack carried out by a person who does not expect to survive it

Statistics:

- 10th leading cause of death in the US for all ages
- There is one death by suicide in the US every 13 minutes
- suicide amongst males in 4x's higher than among females

{Google.com/suicide definition/ suicide statistics}

Depression

Definition:

- A mental condition characterized by feelings of sever despondency and dejection, typically also with feelings of inadequacy and guilt, often accomplished by lack of energy and disturbance of appetite and sleep.

Christina T. Nance

Symptoms:

- feeling unhappy or worthless
- long lasting tiredness or worn out feeling
- self destructive thoughts or actions
- not being able to sleep or sleeping to much
- eating more than usual or not at all
- headaches or feeling anxious
- trouble concentrating or making decisions

Treatments:

- antidepressant medicines
- talking with a therapist, counselor or friend
- eating a good diet
- getting physical exercise or walking 30 minutes a day

Seek care if:

- you have thoughts of hurting yourself or someone else
- call your local emergency service 911
- go to the closes ER
- call the National Suicide Prevention Lifeline: 800-273-TALK (8255)

{google.com/depression definition}

The Letters

Christina T. Nance

The letters to my kids were the hardest.

As I wrote Jayla's letter, I thought about the struggles I had during my pregnancy. I thought about how she was a tiny bundle of joy weighing only 5lbs 3 oz. and couldn't come home if she didn't gain any weight. I thought about how she was a little mini-me in so many ways. I prayed she wouldn't grow up to be just like me. I thought about her fierce attitude, her outgoing/outspoken personality, her creativeness, her everything.

As I wrote Malik's letter, I thought about how everyone told me I wouldn't be nothing but another teen mother living off welfare my whole life. I thought about the thirty-six hours of labor and the forceps they had to use on his big head. I thought about holding him as soon as he was delivered counting his ten little toes and his ten little fingers on his 7lbs 3oz. / 19 ½ inch long self. I thought about the let downs and me not telling him enough how I proud I was of him and how much I loved him.

Was I a good mother to my children?

Did I fail them?

Will they ever find it in their hearts to forgive me?

Will they grow with hatred in their hearts towards me?

Will they suffer from depression as well?

Will they too attempt suicide?

Dear Jayla,
07/21/14

I love you so much, words cannot express how I feel. I know one day in your heart you will find a way to forgive me. Think of all the fun times we had with each other. I will be with you every day.

Love you today, tomorrow and forever more,

Mommy

Dear Malik,
07/21/14

I love you so much. I know one day you will make some girl proud. Respect James and help him with your sister. Know that I am with you every single day. Make me proud son.

Love you today, tomorrow and forever more,

Mommy

The letter to my husband was hard because we always stressed how important communication was in our marriage and I felt I failed him, by not communicating how I was feeling.

As I wrote James's letter, I thought about our wedding day. I reflected back on our vows and how my I witnessed my husband first tears, his tears of joy. I thought about our ups and downs, our smiles and frowns, our everything. I thought about all the chances we had to say "I love you", but didn't. I thought about the times we shared our bed together, but seemed to be complete strangers. I thought about the day he met my son and took him as if he was his own. I thought about the day we signed on our house. I thought about our bond, our union, our everything.

Was I a good wife?

Did he notice me changing and if he did, did he care?

Did he love me like a man is supposed to love his wife?

What did I do wrong?

Will he forgive me?

Will be able to help the kids get through this?

How did this affect him?

Dear James,
07/21/14

I forgive you! I will always love you! I pray you find true happiness. Please remind my kids of me every day. Hug and kiss the. Help them understand. Please forgive me.

Love you today, tomorrow and forever more,

Tina

The letter to my mom was emotional. Although it was short, it was hard to write. I had a lot of unanswered questions, but I no longer wanted answers. I just wanted forgiveness from her. I wanted to feel needed, I wanted my mommy. I needed my mommy. I thought about the time I told her I was pregnant with my first born. I thought about the struggles and sacrifices she went through to provide for my siblings and I. I thought about the arguments we use to have, our ups and downs and regardless of what we went through, she always stood by my side.

Was I the reason she moved?

Would she ever forgive me?

Do she love me?

Will she forgive me?

Did she suffer from depression and kept it away from me?

Dear Mom,
07/21/14

I love you! I will hold you tight! Please forgive
me!

Love,

Tina

My day started off as usual, I stopped and grabbed 4/32 oz. cups of crushed ice with a sausage and cheese toaster sandwich no egg. I didn't even bother grabbing my food out the car once I got to work.

I clocked in at work, grabbed two sodas from the small fridge and logged into my computer. I plugged my headphones into my phone vaguely listening to the music that was playing. I was listening to the Gospel station on IHeart Radio.

I was at work, but I wasn't. Physically my body was there, but mentally and emotionally I wasn't. I received my daily encouraging words from my aunt as I did each day via email.

That day our emails about planning our family trip to Orlando, FL the following year.

The scripture she sent was:

> "I have chosen the way of faithfulness, I have
> set my heart on your laws."
>
> ~Psalms 119:30~

As I looked back on that day and that verse, God WAS speaking to me, I just failed to hear him.

I responded twice that day on email, then I shut my phone off. I wanted no communication from the outside world. My mind was racing. No one existed to me, not my husband, my kids, family, no one.

I thought if I took a walk on my break and clear my mind it would help, but it didn't. Everything in my life seemed like it was falling apart. I couldn't think straight and I was failing at everything in life.

I had got into an argument the night before with my son over something so stupid and my daughter kept nagging me about wanting to read a book to me while I was in the tub and my husband was working late hours and I really felt no one was there to help me.

All I kept hearing as I walked around the parking lot at work was the voices of my kids saying:

> "Mom, can I . . ." or "Mom can this . . ." or
> "Mom, Mom, Mom, Mom, MOM!!!"

I went to the bathroom and splashed some cold water on my face thinking this feeling I was having would go away, but it didn't.

On the way back to my desk, I stopped by the printer and retrieved 4 sheets of blank paper. As I began to write each letter, my tears started falling. It felt as if I was the only one in the room, but I wasn't. No one heard my cries, no one walked by.

I didn't bother clocking out or shutting down my computer. I grabbed my keys and purse and left.

I called James phone and he didn't answer.

I called again and still, no answer.

I need him to answer the phone, I needed someone to talk to and I felt he wasn't there for me.

I cried the whole way home. Once there, I headed to my room and removed my diamond necklace, my earrings and my wedding ring. I placed them on the bed on top of the letters. As I laid the letters down, I kissed each one of them.

I walked downstairs to my son's room, grabbed his pillow and hugged it as if it were his neck. I headed back upstairs to my daughter's room and did the same to her pillow.

I went into the bathroom, grabbed whatever pill bottles I could and tossed them into my purse. As I left my house, I whispered the words "I love you."

I sat in my car long enough to send a text message to my family.

The Message

I sat in my car long enough to send a text message to my family

~*July 21, 2014/3:35pm*~

My dear family,

I love you all unconditionally and I hope one day in your heart you can forgive me. Every day I find ways to encourage others, but I'm really trying to encourage myself.

Mom, I want you to know that I forgive you! I love you!

James, I love you! I also forgive you for not seeing the signs, not listening to my humble cries!

Jayla and Malik . . . mommy loves you sooo much. Please know I will always be with you!

James please give them their letters and comfort them.

I didn't know which direction I was going, I just drove. I almost ran off the road from crying.

I was getting upset because the traffic was backed up on the interstate and my phone wouldn't stop ringing.

There were countless text messages and numerous phone calls pinging on my phone.

The more my phone rang, the more my tears fell. I took the battery out my phone and threw it in my purse.

I drove until I couldn't drive no more. My eyes were swollen from all the crying I had been doing.

I got off on exit 432, Gretna. I saw a hotel and checked in.

> "I would like a room please, top floor" I told
> the man as I handed him my information
> and money.

I had to give the man at the front desk a $25 deposit since I was paying with cash.

I checked in under my maiden name Smith.

I went to the gas station next door and brought a bottle of liquor.

I parked my car in the back of the hotel and headed up to my room.

Once inside my hotel room, I placed the chair under the door and closed the curtains. I removed my clothes, retrieved the bottles of pills and started popping pill, after pill, after pill, after pill.

I removed a notebook from my purse and began to tear blank pages out. I licked each sheet and placed them on the mirrors in the room and bathroom. I remember getting frustrated because the paper kept falling down and wouldn't stick so I turned the lights out in the room.

I couldn't stand the site of myself.

> "You're not perfect TINA! Nobody loves you
> TINA!" I yelled over and over again.

> "You're not perfect! You failed! You failed
> TINA!" I cried.

> "Fuck everyone! Fuck them all! Fuck you
> Tina! You ain't shit!" I continued to cry as
> I took a drink of the bottle of liquor I had.

I wrote more letters to James and my mom wanting to get more off my chest. I had so much I wanted to tell them both.

I wanted them to forgive me,

I wanted to make sure they took care of my kids, my babies.

I wanted them to understand me. I wanted them to want me.

I began to sweat, which was odd because I was freezing.

I was scared.

I couldn't find my cell phone or my purse.

I began to panic.

I could barely open my eyes. I was able to grab hold of the hotel phone.

I dialed my mom cell. It went to voicemail.

I called again.

Voicemail.

I hit the hotel phone and began to cry.

I wanted my mom, I needed my mom.

As I laid on the hotel floor crying, my mind was racing with unanswered questions.

Did I give them my all?

Did they appreciate everything I did for them?

Did I fail them?

Will they ever forgive me?

Was I a good wife?

Did he notice the changes in me?

Did he love me as I loved him?

What did I do wrong?

Was I the reason she moved?

Could she forgive me?

Did she love me?

I got no response.

I felt God didn't hear my humble cries. I felt that HE was mad at me.

I began to pray "Lord please don't let me die."

I tried calling my mom again and got her voicemail.

This time, I left her a message. "Mom, help me please . . ."

I had dozed off.

I jumped to a ringing sound. I laid there for a while trying to figure out where the sound was coming from.

I was gone.

I was on cloud nine.

I was higher than cloud nine.

I heard the ringing again.

This time I was able to grab the phone.

She spoke, her words were soft. She had been crying.

> "Tina, do you know where you are?" she said
> into the phone.

I started to cry.

> "Tina" she called out.

> "I'm sorry momma, I'm sorry, please forgive me." I sobbed.

> "Talk to me Tina, just keep talking to me." She said softly.

My cries had turned into a deep sob.

> "Tina . . ." I remembered as her last words.

There was a knock on the door and before I could get enough strength to respond, the hotel room door was being kicked in.

> "Mam, Mam" a lady said checking me for a pulse.

> "Help me, please help me" I said in low tone with little breathe.

> "We have a black female 25-30, attempted suicide, faint pulse, overdose, nathrologic." The paramedic said.

> "I'm cold" I stated

> "Mam, can you tell me your name? Mam . . ."

God had saved me.

The Check-in Process

When I look back on that day, I ask myself:

How were they able to locate me? I turned my cell phone off and was unable to be located. Was it from the voicemail I left my mother on her cell phone?

What caused my depression? Did I hide it so well that I allowed it to consume my thoughts and take over?

How long have I been suffering from it? Did this start when I was a kid and never noticed it since we never spoke on it?

Can my depression be passed on to my kids? If so, will I notice the signs before it's too late?

Did I inherit this from my mother? From my father? Do either of them suffer from depression?

When I woke up, I was in the emergency room. I had an IV bag in my right arm and blood was being drawn from my left.

They used the IV to flush out my system.

> "You're really lucky they found you when
> they did" said the lady nurse.

I looked around the room trying to focus my eyes on everything that was happening.

> "You have a waiting room full of loved ones,
> but only one can come back" she continued.

"I'm sorry, please forgive me" I cried to no in particular.

The nurse stopped what she was doing and came to my bedside and spoke, "it is okay, there is no need to be sorry, calm down, you're safe now." She said hugging me.

I had dozed off.

There was no stop movement going on in my room. There were police officers, the paramedics and hospital staff. They were asking me all types of questions I could not answer.

They wanted to know if this was my first suicide attempt. Did anyone assist me in my attempt? Did I know my name, my date of birth, todays date? The questions kept coming.

I began to cry. Why was they treating me like I am crazy, of course I know my name, of course I know my date of birth, but the one thing I didn't know was whether it was night or day, Monday or Tuesday.

I had closed my eyes and drifted off to sleep.

I thought I was dreaming when I heard his voice.

"I don't know whether to hug or hit you" he said wiping his eyes.

I turned to look at him.

"Why Tina" he asked.

He was James, my husband.

I began to cry. "I'm sorry, I'm sorry, I'm sor—"

"Why Tina" he asked again.

He held me tight, trying to muffle his own tears.

I turned away from him.

> "Look at me Tina, did you think about your
> kids? Why Tina?" He said in what sounded
> like an angry voice.

I pulled away from him, I was unable to look at him. Unable to face him. I wasn't supposed to see him anymore. The kiss we shared earlier that morning was supposed to be our last kiss, our last eye contact, our last hug, our last everything.

> "Look at me" he demanded

> "No need in beating yourself up, talk to me,
> help me understand" James continued.

I cried.

He cried.

We were interrupted by the nurse.

"Excuse me sir, can we speak to you in the hall?' she asked.

She closed the door behind them. I was trying to figure out what was going on.

A few moments had passed before James returned to the room.

"Tina, I love you" he said kissing me.

"I will let the kids and the rest of the family know you are okay. You get some rest my love." He said kissing my forehead.

I lifted my hands in a confused gesture, trying to figure out what was going on.

"We about to head home and they will call me once they find a place for you to go" he said looking into my teary eyes.

"Huh, wait. What" I asked lifting up out the hospital bed.

"Take me home James, I'm scared. I'm afraid to fall asleep, why can't I go home." I said as I started to cry.

"Calm down, they are going to get you some help Tina. I promise once they let me know where they will be taking you, I will be there, but for now, we have to go." He said.

"I love you, we love you. Get some rest and
we will see you soon." He continued.

"Please don't leave me, please" I cried loudly.

He kissed me, took my personal items from the nurse
and left.

"I'm sorry God please hear me, I'm sorry" I
said through sobs.

Sorry

Definition:

- feeling distressed, especially through sympathy with someone else's misfortune
- filled with compassion
- feeling regret or penitence
- used as an expression of apology
- used as a polite request that someone should repeat Something that one has failed to hear or understand
- in a poor or pitiful state or condition
- unpleasant and regrettable, especially on account of Incompetence or misbehavior

I'm not sure what they put in my IV, but my high was coming down and I was getting sleepy.

I was too scared to fall asleep.

I stared at the wall clock like the time was going to move faster than what it was.

2:37am

2:39am

2:40am

2:41am

I dozed off.

> "Christina, Christina" I heard the lady nurse say.

I turned to face her.

> "We found a place for you. You have to be under observation for 72 hours." She sated as she began to remove the IV from my arm.

> "I'm okay, I want to go home" I told her

> "I understand mam, but this is protocol with a suicide attempt" she said as calmly as she could.

The police officer entered the room and confirmed what the lady nurse had told me. She stated they had found letters at the hotel I had written earlier that raised some concerns and I needed to be under observation.

I turned my back to them both and cried.

The officer told me everything would be okay and left the room.

The lady nurse continued to speak to me.

> "I need you to remove your bra and underwear and put these on" she said handing me a pair of tan looking scrubs and no fall socks.

> "I don't want to go, I just want to go home to my family." I said.

> "Please let me go home, my husband and family will keep an eye on me, I'm okay now, just please let me go home." I cried.

She explained that I will be okay, I will go through a separate entrance from the public and that their medical staff is properly trained. She advised me that she had contacted my husband to let him and the rest of my family know where I would be going.

The clock had read 4:41am when the ambulance finally arrived to take me to the treatment facility.

Once inside the ambulance, I noticed the guy holding a clear bag with my underclothes, paperwork and my cell phone.

> "May I see my phone so I can call my husband" I asked

> "The nurse already called and informed him of your placement" he stated with no emotion.

> "Okay" I said softly

The ride was long and I was getting sleepy.

> "Can you watch me while I sleep" I said

> "Go ahead mam, I'll keep an eye on you" he responded.

The check in process went okay, I was asked a lot personal questions. I was asked if anyone in my family suffered from Mental Illness.

I looked at the man like he was crazy and said "Mental Illness? NO!!!"

Why would he ask me about Mental Illness, I'm not suffering from any mental illness!!

The guy checking me in allowed me to use my cell phone. I wanted to call my husband, but I couldn't, I was too ashamed.

Once I turned my phone on, I had 64 text messages and 23 voicemails.

I assumed there were more messages based off the conversation.

A few of the messages read:

5;00pm-"I have the kids, where should I take them"

5;00pm-"they're asking for their mom"

5;01pm-"should we meet somewhere"

5;02pm-"yes"

5:02pm-"where"

5;03pm-"the house maybe"

5;04pm-"yall find her"

5:04pm-"is someone keeping the rest informed"

5:04pm-"please don't let the kids be around when ya'll talk. Don't get them upset until we know something"

5:05pm-"where are we supposed to leave them, so we can talk"

I couldn't read anymore. I couldn't control my tears. What have I done? My kids!!

Tears began to fall from my eyes.

I noticed a message from a number I did not recognize.

> 8:41pm-"Tina you can talk to me or my husband. I don't know what is wrong, but please think of your children and keep God first. Everybody is worried sick about you."

Who was this message from and how did they know what was going on with me? How did they get my number?

Something about that text message made me say out loud:

> "Pull it together Tina, God saved you"

Here it was a complete stranger to me at the time telling me her and her husband are there for me and to keep God first.

God was still showing me favor when I let him down.

My tears couldn't stop, they wouldn't stop.

> "Everything will be okay" the guy said as he escorted me to the secured area.

Once I arrived to the secured area I had to remove the scrubs the hospital gave me and put theirs on. I also had to remove my hair tie and get a full body search. I was given a pair of tan no slip socks and was escorted to a room . . . my room.

There was a thin twin mattress, a thin sheet, a thin blanket and a small pillow. I stood by the door scared to walk in all the way.

I laid down on top of the blanket and cried some more.

> "Breakfast is at 7" the guy said as he closed the door.

The room I was in was at the end of the hall. There were windows in there, but they were locked.

I could hear other people in their rooms, they were crying, yelling or throwing things at the door. One guy even threw his thin mattress into the hallway. He had peed on it.

I got up and glanced out the windows. I said a prayer.

> "My God, I humbly come to you asking for your forgiveness. I will never question your work, but why me? Please help me understand why this is happening to me? Did I do something wrong? Did I fail you? I am not blaming you for my choices, but why me?"

Breakfast was served to each party on paper ware with a plastic spoon.

After breakfast, I was allowed to use the community phone until it was time for my evaluation.

I called James.

His tone was calm and mellow. He sounded restless.

> "Your sister flight get in this afternoon." He stated

> "I spoke with your mom, I told her I hadn't heard from you and was waiting on your call" he continued.

> "I'm sorry" I cried

> "Tina, it's okay, stop crying, you have to pull yourself together" he said.

I asked him about the kids and he said he dropped them off at their activities. He did not want to stop their routine until he knew what was going on with me.

My next call was to my mom.

> "Mom, I'm sorry" I sobbed

> "Tina? Tina, everything is going to be okay" she choked.

I could tell she had been crying by the tone of her voice.

> "What are they saying" she asked.

> "I haven't met with anyone yet" I said through sniffles.

We talked for a few more moments and she ended the call saying:

"Tina, know I love you, we love you!"

I returned to the room . . . my room.

I was finally able to fall asleep.

Knock! Knock!

A man poked his head in and said "Christina, Are you Christina?"

I lifted my head and turned towards the door.

"Yes" I responded

"Would you come with me please, I would like to speak with you" he said

He was the therapist.

He asked the same questions he guy did when I checked in. He started the session off by studying me. Studying my body language. He watched my very closely over the tip of his glasses.

"Why are you here" he asked

I looked away.

He wrote a few things down on a notepad he had in his lap.

"Why are you here" he asked again.

I lifted my head and looked him in his eye and whispered "I tried to kill myself"

"I can't hear you" he stated as he wrote something down on his pad again.

"I tried to kill myself" I said a little louder this time.

Tears began to fall, my tears.

"I'm sorry, please let my family know I am sorry" I said

"What you did scared a lot of people you know" the therapist said

He stared at me again.

"Look around you, you don't belong here" he continued.

We spoke for about thirty more minutes. He asked me questions about my child hood. We spoke on my relationship with my kids, my step kids. We spoke on my relationship with my parents and siblings and we spoke on my marriage.

I wanted to keep the conversation going as long as it was directed away from me. I didn't want to talk about me. I wasn't ready to face me. I was afraid of me.

The therapist stepped out the room.

Ten minutes later he returned.

> "Normally there is a seventy-two hour hold, but I am going to release you to your family." He said as he wrote some things down.

I looked up. Did I hear him correctly?

> "Why?" I asked with a confuse express on my face.

> "As I stated earlier, you don't belong here. You need to schedule an appointment with your primary care doctor and continue to see your therapist. You need plenty of rest and take some time off to heal" he stated.

I whispered "thank you Jesus."

Therapist

Definition:

- a person trained in the use of psychological methods for helping patients overcome psychological problems

I knew in my heart I did not belong in no secure area, behind locked doors, without my underclothes on. I was not crazy, I didn't suffer from mental illness. Yes I was a bit stressed out, but who don't get stressed.

I kept telling myself over and over again nothing was wrong with me, I just need some ME time, that's all. I just need to tune the world off for a minute.

I was in total denial that I suffered from any type of mental illness. Not me. I am not mental . . .

I didn't know where to turn. I was always there for everyone, but who was there for me? My family would call me for comfort and encouraging words, but who could I call? I couldn't reach out to them if they were reaching out to me.

The check-out process went fast. I was re-evaluated and given my under garments. Although they had already spoken to James, I still called him.

He told me that my sister and aunt wanted to pick me up and he will get the kids and see me at the house.

I was escorted outside by a staff member and greeted by sister and aunt. I did not care who seen me coming out the main entrance.

I hugged my sister tight and cried on her shoulder. My aunt held the back door of her car open and hugged me as I got inside.

The Aftermath

As I put on my seatbelt, I broke down.

My sister turned around and said "Everything will be okay Tina"

I saw my aunt looking at me through her rear view mirror with hope in her eyes for me.

Before we headed to the house, we stopped at my other aunt house to pick up my car and get my house keys. I could tell that my aunt had been crying as well and again, I was unable to control my tears. My husband and aunt husband went back to the hotel earlier that day to retrieve my car and other personal belongings.

My sister took my car, left and went and got us some food, then meet my aunt and me at my house.

Once we arrived at the house, I asked my sister to remove all medication from the bathroom and discard it.

After a long hot bubble bath and some food, I wanted nothing but rest.

Unfortunately, the way my family is, that did not happen.

A few moments later, my husband, James walked through the door with my kids.

I was unable to look them in the eyes.

The look on my daughter Jayla face tore me up. Her eyes had sadness in them. It was as if she had been crying all day at the center she attends daily. When she say it was actually me, her eyes lit up, she came and hugged me so tight not wanting to let go. She cried on my shoulders and kept telling me over and over how much she loved me.

The look on my son Malik face was unexplainable. It was as if he felt he was the cause of me leaving and it was up to me to reassure him it was not. He came over and hugged me and cried as well.

My kids were not aware of what had happened with me. They just knew mommy was missing.

How would I ever get enough courage to explain to my kids what I did? How can I tell them day in and day out about staying positive and strive for nothing the best in life when I allowed life to get the best of me?

"What have I done to my kids?" I thought.

"How did I allow myself to do this to them?"
I asked no one in particular.

I went into the room with my husband James and we just hugged and kissed each other. I knew he wanted to say more, but we had guest and he would speak to me later on. He had to be strong for the sake of our kids, but I knew on the inside he was torn.

His face showed no expression.

My family came and went most of the night.

Folks brought food, drinks, deserts, cards, comforting words, etc.

There were lots of tears shed, laughter and stories told.

Family I had not spoken to in months stopped by. In my heart I felt they stopped by to show support, but later on I learned some only to be nosey.

It felt as if they were mourning me as I sat right next to them. It felt like I was at my own repass.

I sat back in the corner of my off white sectional and cried. A cry no one could hear but me. After a while, my cry was no longer silent.

I asked myself:

"What do they think of me?"

"Do they think I'm crazy?"

"Will they watch my every move from this day forward?"

"Who is here because they care? Who is here to be nosey?"

Everyone had cleared out about midnight or so. I was tired, but too scared to fall asleep.

My sister had got the kids off to bed. She helped my husband clean the house and got herself situated for the night.

Before I went to my bedroom, I thanked my sister for traveling all the way her to be by my side and help my James with our kids.

She told me:

> "When I got your text, I had to re-read it, I thought my eyes were playing tricks on me. She said she was just having a training with her soldiers about Suicide Prevention and training them on ACE (ask, care, escort) How to look for the signs."

She continued on say:

> "I dropped everything I was doing and broke down crying and kept calling your phone back to back. I went online and found the first flight I was able to get."

We hugged each other, told one another we loved them and I headed towards my bedroom.

Finally James and I were able to have some alone time.

I knew that my husband wanted to be alone with me as soon as he got home with the kids, but he knew that my family was going to be there and do as much as they can to help him.

He held me so tight that night. He would not let go. Every time I moved, he moved. Every time I got up to go to the bathroom, he got up to make sure I was okay.

I could not sleep. I tossed and turned all night long.

3:15 am I walked downstairs to my son's room.

3:17pm I walked upstairs to my daughter's room.

I did not disturb their sleep, I just stood by their door and admired them. I shed a few tears and admired them.

I woke my sister up with my crying. She asked me what was wrong and I told her nothing.

She said:

> "Tina it is okay, let it out, but you have to stop keeping stuff in."

I just cried.

She sat up with me. James came in the hall to see what was going on and I told him nothing. I assured him I was okay and to go back to bed. He would not go without me.

I hugged my sister again and went to bed.

5:10 am I was up again, unable to sleep.

This time I put my pink running shoes on and walked up to the field to clear my mind. Two laps in, I noticed my husband walking along side me asking what was wrong.

> "How could I allow myself to get to this point in my life?"

"What was I thinking?"

He just held me and told me everything was going to be okay.

We walked back down to the house.

When we got there, my sister was up waiting for us. She was on the phone with my mother.

My mom was in Atlanta headed to the airport to head here. She wanted to speak to me.

> "Tina, I will be there by noon. Once I get there we will talk and you will I see to it you get some rest. I love you"

James and I returned to our room and fell back asleep.

Later on that day, my mom had arrived. I was not ready to face my mother. I had so many emotions running through my mind when it came to my mom.

I felt in my heart when my mom moved to Atlanta, she had abandon me. No matter how old I am, I still needed my mom. I WANTED my mom.

I needed to hear that she loved me. I WANTED to hear that she loved me.

I needed to know that she was there for me. I WANTED to know that she was there for me.

I really needed my mom. I WANTED her.

I knew my mom was there for me, just not when I wanted her to be. I felt she did not need me anymore. As much as I complained, I no longer felt wanted. I knew my mother loved me and that she was only a phone call away, but the inner child in me wanted my mother.

I had so much I needed to tell her, so much I WANTED to tell her and I never did. I wanted to apologize to my mom for all the wrong things I have done, I wanted my mom to tell my mom that I love her and have the upmost respect for her, I wanted to tell my mom that it was okay to let go of me because I now had my own family, but when my mom walked through the door, I wanted nothing but to hug my mom.

Tears fell from both our eyes. She grabbed me. She hugged me and took me to my room. She closed the door and we talked. I gave my mom the letter I had wrote her and we talked some more.

> "You know I am about to put a stop to all this traffic and you are about to rest. You about to take a hot bath, take these meds and rest" she stated.

My mother, sister and the rest of my family was a big help to my husband during that time and thereafter.

Survivor

Definition:

- a person who survives, especially a person remaining alive after an event in which others have died
- the remainder of a group of people or things
- a person who copes well with difficulties in their life

{google.com/definition of survivor}

Seconds turned into minutes, minutes turned into hours, hours turned into days, days turned into months.

Just like an addict in an AA meeting keeping track of their sober days, I kept track of my days. My survival days.

No longer able to afford therapy for myself, I leaned on the only reliable therapist I knew and that was God.

Therapy provided a sense of comfort speaking to someone who did not know me enough to judge me. My job provide a number you could call in anonymously to speak to someone. It was okay at first, but that started to add to my depression. I felt like each time I called in, I spoke with someone different, but I was asked the same questions over and over.

Every morning I thanked HIM for allowing me to see another day. Every day was a struggle. I was given a second chance at life. My faith in God was stronger than ever before and the love I have for myself is amazing.

HE opened my eyes to see certain things that were always there, but I was too blind to see. HE opened my ears to hear the help I was silent to. HE opened my mouth for my cries to escape. HE opened my arms for me to stretch them to him. HE helped me find ME.

Never once did I stop to think that my actions would affect my love ones more than it affected me. Everyone was so concerned about my wellbeing, but no one really stopped to ask my kids or husband how it affected them.

How many sleepless nights did they have?

Did they receive therapy afterwards?

Will they be able to trust me on my own?

My son Malik had anger built up in him towards my husband, thinking he was the cause of my disappearance, but he wasn't.

My son had therapy once a week for his behavior and I asked his therapist at the time if we should tell him and he advised me that it could go one or two ways. He stated that Malik could use it to his advantage and use it as a weakness towards me or he can grow from it and change his ways and ask himself "what role did I play in my mother's depression?"

I decided to tell my son a week before I spoke to my church family about my attempt. I wanted my son to hear from me and no one else what had happened to me. I needed to have a one on one with him and look him into his eyes and explain to him in full detail about everything. I also advised my son that if he ever felt down or needed someone to talk I am here for him.

I explained to Malik that he no longer needed to have anger towards his step dad James because he was not the cause of my attempt.

My daughter was too young to understand what was really going on, so to this day, I have not told her. As time go on and I feel she can understand what is going on, I will have the same conversation with her as I had with her brother.

It took my husband almost a year to tell me how he felt. He was afraid that his honest answer would make me feel a certain type of way, but I needed him to be honest with me. He told me that I was selfish for trying to end my life. He told me I did not think about the affect it would have had on my kids that I would have left them all with unanswered questions. He stated that everyone would look to him as if he was the reason I took my life and that even to this day he still feels that people think that. He felt that I did not love him enough to come to him and let him know that I felt I had too much on my plate.

I . . . I did not know what to say to my husband. Everything he had said was the truth. I did not stop to think about any of those things.

I was tired of trying to be the perfect mom, I was tired of trying to be the perfect wife, I was tired of trying to be the perfect sister, daughter, niece, everything. Everyone always called me with stuff and I would uplift them, but who was uplifting me? Who could I call and talk to when everyone else had their own issues to deal with?

I was not perfect and I wasn't able to help everyone, like I wish I could have.

No Longer Hiding

A lot of folks assumed, many gossiped, but no one came to me directly.

I lost a few friends, but I didn't dwell on it. To me, they weren't a true friend to leave me at my darkest hour.

I felt I could tell MY STORY, MY TESTIMONY better than anyone.

On day 99, I decided to make it known to all my family and friends via social media. But first I needed to speak with my husband. I needed, I WANTED his support 100% before I did do. He told me he supports me with everything.

My post read:

~Feeling grateful~ October 30 at 8:17pm*Omaha, NE

#mytestimony

Tomorrow will be day 100 . . .

That means a lot to me. These past 99 days have been the toughest of MY life! I have cried, laughed, lost and gained.

July 21st changed MY life in a way that only God can judge ME on. EVERY DAY is a Struggle.

I attempted suicide on this day. I had given up all hope and dreams and asked my family and close friends to watch over MY kids and help them understand. I allowed

SATAN to get the best of ME! Just when I thought I saw the light on the other side MY GOD stepped in and held ME!

I had everything any woman could ask for . . . A big family, my own house, a nice job, a husband, 2 beautiful kids, travel when I want to . . .

SO what would allow ME to stoop so low?

Many ask . . .

Life!

Not sure how my family that did not know what happened that day or my friends would react, I hit post.

The response I received was PRICELESS!

More than a handful of my friends told me they wanted me to know how much my testimony spoke to them. They told me that it was powerful and they would have never known.

Sharing my testimony was not to gain sympathy from anyone or allow someone room to judge me, it was simply to give awareness on Mental Illness and Suicide Prevention.

I told my friends that my outer appearance may seem perfect, but on the inside I was crying out for help. I was too scared to say I needed help.

I had to keep telling myself over and over again that it is okay to mess up. It is okay to fail in life. There called learning paths. With those learning paths you can keep moving forward in life or you can just stop.

I like to think of MY learning paths as obstacles. When you go through obstacle courses, you face challenges and at the end of each challenge you receive an award. At the end of the obstacle of your own learning paths, the award is LIFE.

Suicide is real. Mental Illness is real. Suicide has no color. Mental Illness has no color. Suicide has no age limit. Mental Illness has no age limit.

I reached out to different organizations in the Omaha area to get information about Suicide Prevention and Mental Illness Awareness in the black community. I was very surprised that there was not many.

I later learned that there was a program to become a Peer Support Specialist in the Omaha area. I did some research on the program and reached out to obtain the proper information.

I got in touch with a lady name Carole Coussons de Reyes, who is the administrator for the Office of Consumer Affairs Division of Behavioral Health and Human Services. She listened to my TESTIMONY and invited to come and speak to her colleagues.

At first I was scared to share my TESTIMONY with complete strangers, but I told myself this is something that needs to be done to bring awareness to my community, the black community.

From their facial expressions, I knew I had touched them. Before I left, each person gave me their contact information along with other organizations to reach out to. Words cannot express how thankful I was and still am to have had that experience.

I could no longer face my worst enemy. I could no longer stand being around my worst enemy. I would avoid my worst enemy every chance I got. I would avoid walking in front of a mirror. My worst enemy was ME! I was MY #1 enemy.

As I look back on that I am able to answer a lot of my own questions. I realized that many did stop by because they cared, a few to be nosey and others didn't even know why.

I now know that although my family and friends called me for encouragement, we were actually encouraging each other in our own special way.

I now know that I have two beautiful kids, Jayla and Malik look up to me every single day and they depend on me.

I now know that I am loved by my family.

I now know that my husband James is my #1 supporter and he loves me unconditionally.

I now know that I have a purpose here on this earth.

I now know that God loves me, a sinner, a survivor, a suicide survivor.

I lost a few friends and family too, but I am okay with that. If they cannot stand with my through my darkest, weakest moments in life, then I do not want them standing next to me at my strongest moment. (No love lost)

I no longer want to keep my door closed. I am tired of hiding behind my depression. I want to break the cycle and reach out for help. I want my humble cries to be heard.

I would not change any obstacles I been through that lead up to July 21st, 2014, but the obstacle of my suicide attempt. I will continue to be the one others can turn to for encouraging and I will continue to strive to be the best mother, wife, daughter, sister, niece and friend I can. I now know that God allows us to go through our own storms for a reason that is not known to us. I now know that HE will NEVER put more on us than we can bare.

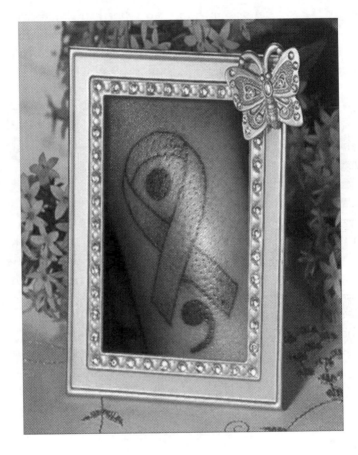

July 21st, 2015

On this day many would have stopped and had a moment of silence in remembrance of me, but God had other plans.

Today I stand tall and speak loudly so my voice can be heard amongst my community, the black community in educating them on Mental Illness and Suicide Prevention.

On this day last year at 3:35 pm I attempted suicide. I sent a text to my family asking them for forgiveness and to help my husband with my kids. I had allowed myself to get to a low point in my life, where I was afraid to ask for help with my depression fearing that someone would think about me.

Words cannot express how blessed and thankful I am of my support system. You ALL know who you are. I love you all unconditionally!

I am a survivor, a suicide survivor! 365 days strong!

I made it!!!!

No one but GOD!!!!

Philippians 4:13: "I can do ALL things through Christ that strengthens ME"

They say most suicide attempters will attempt again within 90 days. Not ME. The thought crossed my mind many times, but my support system was strong, my GOD was stronger. I made it. I am a living testimony that God can and will lift you from your darkest moment.

Even when you want to give up on yourself, don't! God is standing next to you. HE will push you to the edge, it is up to you to trust and believe that he will catch you. This will be YOUR test.

I personally cannot speak on the statics, I am just thankful I did not become one. I struggle with depression daily and on the days I forget to take my medicine (Citalopram 20 mg), I feel down but on the days I do take it, I am okay.

I am no longer afraid of what others think of me. I no longer worry about who is standing with me or against me.

Just like an addict keeping track of their sober days, I too keep track of mine . . .

. . . I am a survivor, a suicide survivor.

I continue to stand tall and one day my voice will be heard.

I reached out to a few family members and two close friends and asked them:

If you are willing can you please send me your reaction or feelings when you found out about my attempt?

Message 1: My stomach literally dropped to the pit of my stomach, then came the tears. I was in shock . . . how did this happen? Why didn't I notice something was wrong? She's one of the best mother's I and friends I know . . . I didn't want to hear or believe this.

Message 2: I can't say I felt a certain way about your suicide attempt, because my emotions were all over the place . . . when I found out about your attempt I was sad. I didn't/don't understand why anyone would not want to be here . . . because I suffer from depression and low self-esteem, I'm constantly fighting to stay strong, battling to keep on keeping on. So I was mad that decided to "give up" . . . I was happy, overcome with joy and relieved when you were found. Thank God that HE had other plans for you!

Message 3: I was in the hospital crying uncontrollably once the kids left and went to my mom's house. I felt helpless because I couldn't leave the hospital to look for you. I was also hurt and upset that it was on my birthday, but more worried about you and if you were okay.

Message 4: scared, I knew right away what you were going to do from my training . . . I called you seconds after you sent that text because I knew what of letter it was, I called the family and told them to go look for you!

Message 5: Scared, hurt, mad and upset

Message 6: My first reaction was disbelief then panic I couldn't or wouldn't allow myself to think that you would do something like this, it was totally out of character for you. My next emotion was confusion because I didn't understand what would make want to leave your family, everything seemed to be going good, but I am just an outsider. My next emotion was anger because to me this was a attention seeking game you were playing then I felt relief and a sense of calmness when you were found.

Message 7: I received the call and I thought about every time we talked and asked if you were okay, you would say yes, God won't put more on me than I can handle I said your so right and I am here anytime you need me. I just didn't think you was capable of it, I mean your kids brought you so much life. I was shocked, sadden. I was numb. Unsure if you were alive or not, thoughts going through my head, I could of helped her, I failed her. I lost my friend. This whole time she was asking for help, I just ignored her, I just broke down.

Message 8: I was in total shock to begin with, I then became frighten and scared not knowing if you were okay!! When you were finally found there was a sense of relief but still on edge. As the night went on, I started to grow angry, asking how she could do something like this! She has kids!! Don't she know she is loved? Don't she know she is needed?!?! Her kids need her, our family needs her. I need her!!! Then I had to come to the realization that I can't rationalize someone else struggles and demons. We all handle things differently. Then I said a silent prayer and my feelings were I am just thankful that God kept you here with us. Finally I was at the state of graceful . . .

Message 9: My first initial reaction was panic as a mother knowing you will be okay and uneventful in your attempt.

Trying to figure out what led you to do something like this. There is always quilt as a mother was there something I did wrong to have made her get to this point. Am I a bad mother? Once I knew you were okay I switched gears to anger, mad you would try something so "stupid". I thought that was some dumb shit "white people" do. We as black folks don't commit suicide. Then I went through the thought process of disbelieve that my child is dealing with some mental issues. Then it is trying to understand what it she's going through is and is there something I could have done wrong to prevent it. Is part of it dealing with the animosity she has towards me? Did she blame me for her attempt or is she really facing the real issues that she have going on in her life? I asked myself if I could have been a little more affectionate as a mother. A better listener as opposed to do as I say not as I do as I am the parent and therefore what I say goes. Could I have done things different to improve our relationship?

Their responses not only gave me closure, but it also made me aware that I am loved. I am needed and that I do have a purpose in life. Their responses told me that I have a positive effect on them and that we all motivate each other in our own special way.

It also made me aware that I do stand alone in depression and that my family and friends have hidden behind mental illness and we all need help.

I no longer want my family and friends to hide behind closed doors, I no longer want them to feel ashamed of their illness and seek proper help. I want to save them like God saved me.

~Healing isn't something that happens overnight, it takes time. Healing starts with you. In order to heal, you must first forgive yourself~

Notes

Notes

Notes

Notes

Notes

About the Author

Christina T. Nance resides in Omaha, Nebraska, with her husband, James E. Nance Sr., and their two kids, Malik and Jayla. She is currently taking online courses at Kaplan University, working on her associate's degree in applied science and human service. Christina attends Fellowship Christian Center. She is a pillar of her family and soon to be pillar of her community.

If you would like to reach Christina, you may do so at mystorymytestimony@yahoo.com or at https://www.facebook.com/christina.nance.395

Printed in the United States
By Bookmasters